W9-CVU-358

CHURCH USHERS' MANUAL

A Handbook for Church Ushers
and all Others who would Pro-
mote the Spirit of Fellowship in
the House of God ∴   ∴   ∴

By
WILLIS O. GARRETT, D. D.
Pastor, First Presbyterian Church, Miami, Fla.

SIXTEENTH PRINTING

NEW YORK   CHICAGO
Fleming   H.   Revell   Company
LONDON   AND   EDINBURGH

Copyright, 1924, by
FLEMING H. REVELL COMPANY

Printed in the United States of America

New York: 158 Fifth Avenue

FOREWORD

FEW forms of Christian service are adorned with loftier privileges or ladened with weightier obligations than that of ushering in the Church of Christ. Whosoever is honoured with this office, should immediately declare himself for maximum efficiency.

The usher is the Church's official representative of the host spirit—a side of Church expressional life which in too many cases has been neglected and has resulted to the serious detriment of the Church as a soul-gripping institution.

The usher cannot bear the whole burden of friendliness, but it is his privilege to stand in the gap to perform for the Church that which the Church as a whole cannot do for itself.

Some men do well in this capacity without special training, but few there be who may not do better by giving the matter careful study. This, along with prayer and practice, will work wonders for any one who earnestly desires to be a good host in the house of God.

The purpose of this Manual is to present in brief form some of the principles of ushering and of welcoming strangers at church services. It is little more than suggestive, but if rightly used, may give inspiration to all who are willing to be helped. At least it should aid to a better appreciation of the importance of this work.

"Let brotherly love continue: be not forgetful to entertain strangers; for thereby some have entertained angels unawares" (Heb. 13: 1, 2).

W. O. G.

Miami, Fla.

CONTENTS

CONTENTS

I

THE USHER

I. *Starting Right*

1. The very foundation of efficiency in this work lies in having a right mental attitude toward it. Start right by seeing it in its large proportions. Weigh its values. Ponder over its possibilities. Be impressed with its importance. Hold it in high esteem.

2. Think of it primarily as real Christian service. It is Kingdom work. You are working under Divine orders. Take this as your working motto: " I serve the Lord Christ." As you repeat it to yourself over and over again, the Spirit will direct you as you turn your attention to a guest.

3. Resolve to give it the best that is in you. Measure up to your opportunity. Magnify the office with a whole-hearted service. " And whatsoever ye do, do it heartily as unto the Lord and not unto men: knowing that of the Lord ye shall receive the reward of the inheritance: for ye serve the Lord Christ " (Col. 3: 24).

4.   You are receiving guests in the Church of Christ.   It is of utmost importance that Christ has first place in your own heart.

5.   Constantly recall that all Christian work is accomplished by the Holy Spirit.   He works through human instrumentality.   Therefore at the very start, surrender yourself to Him and give Him a chance to work wondrously through you.   Mingle prayer with your service.   Get on to your knees and actually talk to God about this.   Consciously turn your thoughts often to Him while performing your duties.   Trust and obey Him and your deeds will count eternally.

II.   *The Usher as Host*

(A) MEETING THE GUEST, OR THE POINT OF CONTACT:

1.   Frequently remind yourself of the fact that the way in which things are done is often more important than the things themselves. This is true of church-ushering.

2.   Present a neat personal appearance. First impressions count much.   A well-groomed host appeals to observant people, while one who is careless in this regard is oft-times repellent.   Not that one should be fas-

tidious or fussy about his dress. Overdoing it is almost as bad as the other extreme. Neat, tasteful simplicity is what is wanted.

3. Conduct yourself with an air of cultured dignity. This does not mean that you show stiffness or haughtiness, but merely that you go about your duties in such a way that others may perceive that you have an appreciation of the importance of your office. Note carefully that we do not say, " the importance of yourself."

4. Do not entertain the idea that you have been chosen as an usher for your own pleasure or that the church may show you off to the guests. It is possible that you may have a pleasant time and also claim a certain amount of admiration while you are engaged in your work; but this will be incidental. You have been chosen because your fellow church members believe you know how to show the host spirit. Your duty is to make people comfortable. Do not let self become mixed up in this or you will be a failure.

5. Let your every expression convey the idea of friendliness. Without this you will never rank high as an usher. Put your heart into your service in such a manner that your

guest will see and feel it. Envelop him in an atmosphere that will melt him into friendliness. Warm his heart at the very threshold.

6. Shabby treatment at the church door will put many people into the strange mood of expecting shabby treatment from the pulpit. It is a common observation that what a person looks for he generally finds. Play fair with your pastor. Do not spoil his auditors before he has a chance at them.

7. Greet your guest by looking into his face. Generally a pleasant smile will claim one in response. If it does, you have done much toward putting him in a mood for making the best of all your church has to offer. At times it may be proper and profitable to speak a friendly word and sometimes to offer the hand before conducting him to a seat. You will find some few men who will respond encouragingly to a hand laid upon the shoulder as you inquire their preference in seating. On the other hand, to some, this is very distasteful. Your guest is a human being; a personality. Meet him as such.

8. Whenever you know the names of the people to whom you are ministering, make use of them. People like to be recognized and to

be called by their names. " Good-morning, Mr. Brown, may I show you to a seat? " That is the kind of talk that Mr. Brown likes. With this in mind, an efficient usher will try to discover and retain in his memory the names of guests who are occasional worshipers. Even though he may have had no formal introduction, he is privileged as host to address them by name. Let him step up to such an one and say, " Mr. Brown, I believe? We are glad to have you with us. May I show you to a seat? " That is the kind of treatment that will make Mr. Brown a regular worshiper.

9. A warning against undue familiarity may not be out of place. Be friendly without intruding yourself upon your guest to any degree of offense. Use judgment and tact. People are different. Study each guest with a view to pleasing.

10. Do not assume a patronizing air. Be manly. Be sincere. Be friendly from the heart outward.

11. Never embarrass a guest. It doesn't matter how wrong he may be, in what he does or does not do. Under no circumstance let him know that you think he is wrong. You are not there to administer discipline, but to

make him comfortable. Circumstances and conditions do not alter your duty. If you feel that he does not deserve consideration, your part is to control your feelings and play the part of a good host.

12. Make no exceptions in the display of courtesy, even when guests are unresponsive and cold and when they meet your proper advances with a rebuff. It may require a special effort on days when your own physical and mental condition is subnormal; at times when you are most susceptible to irritation. It will not be hard, however, if you say to yourself, " I serve the Lord Christ."

13. Guard against favoritism. Show no more attention to rich than to poor. Receive the latter with the same Christian cordiality. If these seem ill at ease because of the contrast in dress and condition, take special pains to make them comfortable; and especially let them know that they are most welcome. " Be ye of the same mind one toward another. Mind not high things but condescend to men of low estate " (Rom. 12: 16). The same should be said regarding showing favoritism to friends.

14. Steer clear of ruts. Do not handicap your usefulness by being satisfied with any-

thing which might be made better. Keep growing. Do not say the same thing to every one. Do not call every man " Brother " or " Friend." Be original. Do things differently. It may not be easy at first, but a little determination and practice will bring results.

(B) SEATING THE GUEST:

1. Study your room. Know where every available seat is. As soon as you have seated one party, determine where you will place the next. Be prepared before the guests arrive. It is embarrassing for one to be kept standing midway up the aisle while the usher frantically searches for a seat.

2. It is well enough for you to have your own ideas as to where people should be seated, but do not forget that your principal duty is to make them comfortable. If their manner or words lead you to think that they are particular about where they are to sit, quietly ask if they have any preference. However, do not make the mistake of asking everybody. Most people will prefer your own decision.

3. Generally speaking, the audience should be seated well forward. This needs special consideration when the attendance is small in

comparison with the seating capacity of the room. It is a great relief to the speaker to have his auditors close to him. Most people, if handled tactfully, do not object to being seated in the center or even near the front of the room. It is a great deal better for the usher to take them forward at the time of their entrance than to have the speaker beg them to come forward later in the service.

4. When, on any occasion the audience is very small, the usher can, with tactful handling, seat the people in such a way as to give the impression that many more are present than is actually the case. Instead of seating them close together in one or two sections of the room, endeavour to scatter them about, putting very few in each pew. The impression which can thus be gained is valuable. It is a matter of useful psychology in which not only the audience is affected, but the speaker as well. Of course judgment should be exercised in this; for the suggestion is of value only up to a certain point.

5. There is a special reason why strangers should be induced to sit toward the front, provided it is not distasteful to them. It gives the home people a better chance to greet them.

They must mingle with them as they go out. After sitting in the back seats it is so easy for them, at the close of the service, to slip out without having received much attention.

6. When practical, seat strangers in pews occupied by church members. It is a little more like being taken into the church family life. If occasion permits, it is well to introduce one to the other.

7. It is a safe rule to select front seats for elderly people. However, even here you must be observant; for, many in advanced years are unimpaired in hearing and prefer other locations. Keep your eyes open. Don't be handicapped by a rule.

8. People carrying ear trumpets or those who otherwise show signs of deafness, should have the privilege of seats close to the speaker. They should be placed in front of him and not at one side. If the church is so fortunate as to be equipped with special instruments to enable the deaf to hear, seat your guest where one can be used.[1] Be careful to see that the in-

[1] The best instrument with which the author has had experience is the Church Acousticon, manufactured by the Dictograph Sales Corp., 580 Fifth Ave., New York City.

strument is properly adjusted and that the principles of its use are fully explained.

9. Watch your step. Do not walk too rapidly. Some ushers give the appearance of running a foot race. It does not look well to run away from your guest. Keep but a pace or two in front of him.

10. If a guest is feeble or walks with difficulty, or seems near-sighted, it is proper for you to offer your arm in assistance: especially should you do this if there are steps to be encountered.

11. During prayer, the reading of the Scriptures or the rendition of special musical numbers, all newcomers should be quietly detained in the vestibule or at the door. To escort them to seats at such a time is to disregard proper church decorum to the disturbance of all who are worshiping, as well as of those who are speaking or singing.

12. When seats are limited in number, see that each pew is seated to capacity. Sometimes people spread themselves over more than their entitled share. A friendly manner and a courteous suggestion usually makes room for another without giving offense.

13. When rearrangements are to be made

to admit another person to the pew, the usher should personally attend to the matter, remaining on the ground until the change has been made. Under no circumstances should he merely direct a newcomer to such a pew and then leave him to push in as best he may.

14. Always conduct your guest to his seat. Never direct him. A pointing finger is a mark of a poor usher. It is not to be considered as a help, but as a hindrance in ushering.

15. There will be times when you will need all your wits. Special occasions will bring crowds. If seats are at a premium, they may be pushing crowds. If you are to master the situation, you must have yourself well in hand. When many are waiting to be seated, make it clear how many are to follow you. You may have in a certain section, seats for a definite number of people—two, three, four, as the case may be. Do not start off heading a procession of a dozen or more. Courteously make it known who are to be escorted and who are to remain until you return. You will save much confusion and embarrassment.

16. Another experience which calls for presence of mind is to have your guest slip into a seat of his own choosing, allowing you

to continue up the aisle alone. Do not make the mistake of showing any displeasure at this. Accept the situation gracefully. Do not take it as a personal affront. It really is not a serious matter. If there is any change in your expression, let it be nothing more than a smile. This will put everybody at ease.

17. Some time when you are engaged or somewhat off your guard, a guest may pass you unobserved and timidly start up the aisle searching for a seat. If you discover that this has happened, go quickly to his side and, with grace, play the part of a host. You may be sure it will be well received; and you will likely be looked upon as the proverbial " friend in need." Even if the person is being seated, when first observed, the courteous thing, provided the service has not yet begun, would be for you to go to him and express regret for the seeming neglect. It will show your interest in him and no one can say how great good will grow out of it.

(C) ATTENDING TO THE COMFORT OF THE GUEST:

1. Finding a seat for your guest does not terminate your responsibility. He is your

guest for the entire service. You are tied up to him. Do not forget him.

2. He should have everything he needs for the service; hymn-book, Bible, programs, bulletin, fan, etc., etc.

3. You should always know what hymn has been announced or is being sung. When offering a hymn-book, have it open at the right place. When pressure of duties makes this impossible, you should at least tell him the number of the hymn. The same applies to all other parts of the service in which the congregation participates; for example, the responsive reading. Whenever a special program is being rendered, it will mean much to the guest who has come a little late, if, as you place in his hands the printed program, you indicate the item thereon which is being rendered. Of course after a while he could find it for himself, but your action will be one more proof that yours is a church " that cares." Little courtesies make a good host.

4. If you have any reason to think that one whom you have seated is uncomfortable, seek to discover the reason and endeavour to remedy it. He may be sitting in a draft; or possibly he would appreciate having a near-by

window opened; or having a fan placed in his hands. It may be a case of an overcrowded pew or some similar situation just as easily met. If he suffers neglect in any of these particulars, your good treatment of him upon his entrance will be largely discounted.

5.   Of course it would be unwise to be running around asking each person if he is comfortable. That would be a good way to make some people uncomfortable. Usually, in such matters the state of one's feelings is indicated by certain signs which are very close to the surface. Generally, to keep informed, you will need no more than your eyes. Of course you will have to keep them open.

6.   Special effort should be made, when attending to his comfort during the service to attract as little attention as possible, lest others be disturbed, to the embarrassment of your guest.

(D) THE AFTER TOUCH:

1.   The pronouncement of the benediction does not necessarily mean that the usher's work is done. It may be just well begun. The true host not only greets his guest upon his arrival and looks after his pleasure and comfort while

he remains, but he also shows for him a friendly concern at his departure. The "farewell" may mean as much as the initial greeting. When it is lacking, one's hospitality may be thought incomplete.

2. In many cases real good can be accomplished by speaking a word to the guest as he passes down the aisle or through the doorway: *i. e.*—"Mighty glad to have had you with us this morning." "Hope you will come again." "I understand we shall have something good here to-night." "Hope you enjoyed the service." "Going to look for you next week." "Would you like to meet our pastor?" "We have a fine church plant here; I wonder if you care to look it over?" All of this means attention, which reaches the heart. It wins.

3. This will prove a favourable time for gleaning information which may add to the greater usefulness of the church. Have your book and pencil ready for names and addresses of prospective members; to make note of cases of the sick and troubled who would appreciate the pastor's attention and of any other facts which your pastor would be glad to have.

4. Should it ever happen that a visitor whom you have seated with others has re-

ceived from them some rebuff or sign of in-
hospitality, you must make a special effort to
overcome the effect of such treatment. Get in
touch with him at the close of the service and
express your regrets at the occurrence. As-
sure him that it was not typical of the general
church life. Extend a warm invitation for
him to return at any early date; and unhesi-
tatingly promise him a more pleasing reception. No loss of dignity ever accompanies the
frank acknowledgment of a mistake.

5. The highest service one can do for another is to lead him to Christ. As an usher,
you will have many opportunities for this kind
of service. You will look into the faces of
many who will crave a personal word about
their soul's salvation. What an opportunity
you have to follow up the evangelistic plea of
the pulpit! You will find when speaking to
individuals about the church services that it is
not a far step to the matter of their own relationship to Christ and His Church. Make it
a rule that you will speak to at least one person
every Sunday, and to more if possible. Put
prayer into it and you will be surprised what
God will do through you. The true host gives
his best to the guest. This is the Church's best,

—eternal life in Christ. This is the "after touch" that extends through eternity.

III. *The Usher and His Co-Workers*

(A) RELATIONS TO THE HEAD USHER:

1. Be a good soldier. Respect the commands of the Head Usher. If he stations you in an obscure place, do not grumble because you would rather be in the central aisle. Make it easy for him to execute his plans, even though this means that many of your own need be changed.

2. Perform your service in the section of the room allotted to you. Do not go into another usher's territory. If you discover a needy spot outside your own, report the same to the Head Usher and let him direct his forces as seems best to him.

3. Back him up by being dependable. Keep your word or promise at any cost. Always remember that he is counting upon you. Be conscientious; for "Ye serve the Lord Christ."

4. Being on time in this work is always considered a mark of efficiency. Your chief will probably lay great stress upon this. If this means reporting for duty twenty to thirty minutes before the commencement of the serv-

ice, do not look upon it as a hardship; but respond to his wishes with a willing and a persistent fidelity.

5. If you find that for good reasons you cannot be at your post of duty, notify your chief at the very earliest possible moment so that he can fill your place with a substitute. Do not fail him at this point.

6. Help your superior officer to bring the standard of the work to as high a point as possible. Study the whole problem. Seek for fruitful ideas and pass them on to him with promptness. However, do not dictate or indulge in uncharitable criticism.

7. One of the hardest things the Head Usher has to do is to make changes in his working force. He sometimes finds men better qualified than some already serving him, yet he hesitates to make the change because so many men take it as a personal injury to be superseded by another. You can help him much by yielding to his judgment in the interest of the church. Make it easy for him to perform his duty in this regard.

(B) RELATIONS TO HIS FELLOW USHERS:

1. It is of the highest importance that a

good spirit shall exist between all who are engaged in this work. Let nothing suggestive of jealous rivalry ever appear. " Be kindly affectioned one to another; in honour preferring one another."

2. Be especially thoughtful and considerate of those who have had little experience in ushering. Encourage them in every way and watch for opportunities to helpfully share your own experience with them.

3. Remember, team work counts. You are yoked with others in a common task. Pull your share of the load without complaint. Do not shirk or shift responsibility.

IV. *The Usher and His Fellow Church Members*

1. The same courtesy should be shown to the fellow church member and regular attendant as to the stranger. Be just as considerate and as eager to make comfortable in one case as in the other. Serve him in every way possible. Be big-hearted and gracious. Kindness cheers the hearts of one's own as much as it does those from without the family circle. Indiscriminate kindness helps to make the home atmosphere.

2. Cultivate the happy art of "missing" people. People are delighted in learning that they have been missed. Therefore, when you observe that regular attendants are absent, make a note of the fact so that upon their return, you can say, " We missed you last week; hope you were not ill; glad to have you back again, etc., etc."

3. It should be your constant aim to foster the spirit of hospitality throughout the entire church. Consider this one of your duties. Everybody helps to make the atmosphere of the church. The important thing is to inspire every one with a common hospitable aim. It is your duty to disseminate the seeds of enthusiasm.

4. The best way to go about this is to talk. Be a promoter. Sell the idea of the hospitable spirit. Talk to individuals, to groups, and to organizations. Convince them that warmhearted friendliness in the church pays big spiritual dividends. Ask individuals how many strangers they spoke to that day. Then show them that they should strive for more activity along this line. At a subsequent date check up on them. You can lead most of them to promise greater fidelity in the matter.

Do this, and you will start something worth while. Some of the icicles in your church will begin melting and folks on the outside will say, " We have found a church that suits us. We feel at home in it. It is a great comfort to worship in such a place."

5. Some of your members will need to be constantly reminded of this duty. Watch for such before the service. Sometimes they can be spurred up to good work by a reminder such as the following: " Say, Mr. Blank, there are a lot of strangers here to-day. We want you to do your part in giving them a hearty welcome at the close of the service."

6. Give special attention to those members who appear to be lacking in this friendly spirit. If you have observed them treating a church guest in an indifferent manner, endeavour to have a friendly chat with them at some suitable time and tactfully drop some practical hints regarding the church's responsibility for its guests. Relate incidents showing good that has come from simple courtesies. You will find few indeed, who are intractable. Try to make their hearts glow by this recital of the attractive possibilities of church friendliness.

The issue will seldom be in doubt. Most of
them can be led out of selfishness and thought-
lessness into soulful cordiality.

V. *In Conclusion*

We stop where we began. You have a
man's job. There is nothing little about it.
Its possibilities are unlimited. It is worthy
of your best effort; for " Ye serve the Lord
Christ." Determine right here that He is going to have your best. " Study to show thy-
self approved unto God, a workman that need-
eth not to be ashamed."

II

THE HEAD USHER

I. *Vision*

1. Few things are of greater value to any leader than the mental grasp of the possibilities of his work. This is a matter of vision; the ability to understand relative values and to see beyond the actual. It makes for progress. It brings things up to their maximum worth. This is the starting point for you as Head Usher. You must properly esteem its opportunity and the responsibility that is yours. Start out with a worthy vision. The best place for you to obtain this is upon your knees, for after all this is God's work and He is the inspiring leader.

2. It is of real importance that you see this work as true Christian service; as chosen by Christ to lead others in the matter of representing Him as host in His Church. He wants to cheer hearts through friendly interest in order that some may thus be led to find Him as Saviour and that all may worship Him. Do not listen to the suggestion that yours is a small service.

3. You must always, in the performance of your duty, think of yourself as host; and of the visitor as your guest. This is a tender relationship. It calls for heart exercise. Mere perfunctoriness, it matters not how exact it may be, does not make a host. You are required not only to be polite, but to be considerate and to show warm interest. The vision of the host ideal must be before you and your helpers all the time.

4. Think of your guests as worshipers. You, therefore, will desire to receive them and care for them in such a way that they will be attuned for worship and fellowship. It is well to remember that their spiritual activities will sometimes be determined by their mental states and even by their bodily comfort.

5. There is no element in the vision of your work quite so important as that which links each guest with Christ. You will not know, as strangers come to you, whether they are professed followers of Christ or not; but your heart should be moved with desire that such as are not, may, that very day, be led close to Him. Christ yearned over the multitude as " sheep not having a shepherd." Even so, should all who have accepted Him, and

especially those who represent Him, as you and your co-workers are called upon to do,—even so should you yearn and work for their souls' salvation. This evangelistic motive will add spirit and worth to your service.

6. Constantly call to mind that God uses His servants. This will not only keep you humble, but will inspire you with courage. There is no greater assurance of success than the abiding consciousness that God is using you. This calls for the consecration of every talent, absolute trust, and whole-hearted obedience.

II. *Generalship*

(A) ORGANIZATION:

1. Head Usher:

In some small churches the ushers may number not over two. Even in these cases one should be designated Head Usher; for it centers responsibility and assures the church of greater efficiency in receiving guests. All churches should have a Head Usher.

2. Assistants:

If the church is large enough to warrant it, the Head Usher should have one or more special assistants. These might be designated.—

first, second, etc. These are to aid the Head
Usher in any way he may designate. When,
for any reason he cannot be at his post, he
would naturally direct one of these to act in
his stead.

3. Ushers:

(*a*) These should be carefully chosen by the
Head Usher, with a view to their ability and
the church's need.

(*b*) In choosing your workers, always recognize that the first qualification is Christian
character. Then comes ability. You may be
tempted to put ability first. You may argue
with yourself that unless a man has ability
he will never make an usher; it matters not
how good he is. That may be true; but there
is something else to be said. Here is the safe
rule: When possible, pass by both the good
man who lacks ability to learn how to usher
and the able man who is not living true to
Christ.

(*c*) As to the age of the men selected, much
depends upon circumstances. In the smaller
churches you cannot confine yourself to a
single group. Personality should have pre-
cedence over age. A rule is observed in many
churches to use the older men at the morning

service and young men at night. When using young men it might be well to have some older ones to first welcome the guests and then turn them over to the younger men.

(*d*) In some churches in order to put more men to work as well as to protect against making the work arduous, several groups of men may be selected. This permits using one group for morning and another for evening; or one group for one month and then another for a succeeding period. The advisability of this plan depends largely upon local conditions.

(*e*) After you have decided what plan you will follow, carefully determine the exact number of men you will need. Appoint these and no more, but try always to keep the ranks full. This applies to the Reserves as well as to the Ushers. It is not a good thing to let the impression get abroad that anybody and everybody in the church may help in this work if he wants to serve. This is one explanation why some churches have such a difficult time getting anybody to serve. It has a salutary effect to let it be known that it is a picked body of men, and that it is a position of real honour as well as of responsibility.

(*f*) Consult your pastor about the personnel

of your ushering force. Go over the list of members frequently. Keep an up-to-date list of possible candidates. Use new members as well as old. Wherever possible get hold of the man who is not doing anything else in the way of church work. It will do him good and also help you, for he will have more time to devote to the work. Do not overwork those who already have too much to do. Accept the challenge of developing new material.

4. Reserves:

(*a*) This provision for a wider efficiency should be more generally adopted. The idea is to have a list of qualified men, to be known as Usher Reserves, for substitute work and special service. It provides for unexpected emergencies as well as acting as a training class for the inexperienced.

(*b*) It should be understood that to have one's name upon this list is not an assurance of later appointment as a regular usher. The only rule of priority should be ability and fitness.

5. Welcome Committee:

(*a*) In addition to your regular ushers it may be advisable to appoint a special committee of men and women to be stationed in the vestibule or other suitable place for greeting the people as they enter the building. There should not be too many of these on duty at one time, especially if they operate at a common point. You must guard against overdoing this form of hospitality. A visitor might be greatly cheered by a friendly word from one or two, whereas a committee, say of five, might give the impression of professionalism and might make the guest feel as though he had run a veritable gauntlet. However, if this committee be composed of the right number of tactful, whole-souled men and women, it will prove of inestimable value.

(*b*) This committee should be under the appointment and full supervision of the Head Usher. Experience will show that its personnel should be frequently changed so that new faces will greet the guest at later visits. This suggestion likewise provides for putting more people to work.

(*c*) Another way to use this committee is to have its members seated at regular intervals throughout the church. At the close of the service they are to see that the strangers within their sections have special attention. This is one of the best systematic methods of welcoming visitors that have been devised. The protection of the crowd saves one from the mark of professionalism or of the performance of duty by appointment rather than by the spontaneity of heart compulsion. This natural protection of the crowd likewise enables you to put to work wholesome characters who draw back from service that gives them publicity. They can do this work without any one around them, even their friends, knowing that they are serving upon a committee.

(B) PLAN OF WORK:

1. The Head Usher or his assistants should be the first to receive the guests upon their entrance into the auditorium. He gives to these some fitting sign of recognition and welcome. He then turns them over to the friendly attention of his ushers. Frequently, where occasion calls for it, he will add words of direction as to special attention to be shown. As a general rule, he will do no ushering himself; though on occasion he may if he desires. His principal duty, after having received the guest, is to direct the activities of his corps of helpers.

2. If there are several doors of entrance

he must assign his assistants to man each of them. It will be their duty to remain at the doors to receive the guests and turn them over to the helping ushers. These assistants should not do the ushering themselves; lest, while they are absent from their post, a guest enter the church without reception. In some instances in large churches where there are several entrances it is best for the Head Usher to confine himself to no one of them, but to keep in touch with all.

3. Assign definite work to each usher. Mark out his territory with exactness and hold him responsible for the same. Discourage his wandering into the territory of others; and at the same time protect him in his rights with respect to his own.

4. It is true that at a certain time after the commencement of the service very few people will arrive. Do not, however, allow all the ushers to find seats for themselves and become absorbed in the service. There is always the possibility of late comers. They should have attention, both for their own comfort and also for the sake of the congregation, lest disturbance arise because of embarrassed search for seats. The Head Usher should therefore see

to it that some one or more of the ushers remain on duty through the entire service. One person stationed in the vestibule might be able to handle the matter alone. If this prevents participation in the service, a system of rotation might be devised so that this duty would come only occasionally to each man.

5. If on special occasions, such as at early vesper services, you grant to the worshipers the liberty of the house, allowing them to choose their own seats, do not overlook the fact that this will be considered an act of courtesy only so long as they can find seats with ease. As the room fills up you must be prepared to render them assistance. This means that at every public service you must have some of your ushers on hand to represent the church as host. It should also be noted that when this privilege of free choice is to be granted, all guests should be greeted at the door upon their entrance and informed of this fact.

6. All communications with the pulpit, choir, etc., should be made through the Head Usher. It makes a bad impression upon visitors to see various members of the congregation going into the pulpit to speak to the pas-

tor or to place announcements in his hands. Order should be one of the honoured rules of the house of God. By announcement in the printed bulletin and also from the pulpit, the congregation should be informed and trained in this matter. Let it be generally understood that all such communications are to be through the Head Usher or one of his assistants whom he designates.

7. Some churches maintain a guest register in the church parlour or vestibule. This should come under the jurisdiction of the Head Usher. He should assign one person to look after it and to invite guests to inscribe their names.

8. One pleasing feature of church ushering is that it needs very little special material equipment. It is a personal proposition. With a consecrated heart, mind, and body, one is ready for work. The Head Usher should, however, pay some attention to the personal appearance of his helpers. Sometimes it is possible and good to adopt a uniform style of dress. For example, all might wear dark clothes with same style of collar and cravat. In some of our largest city churches all the ushers are groomed with frock coats. In

summer, light trousers with dark sack coats, or white suits give pleasing effects. This matter of uniformity, however, is of small importance and many situations do not call for it. Neatness and cleanliness should, however, be insisted upon. A simple custom followed in many churches is that of each usher's wearing a tiny flower upon his coat lapel. It might be advisable in some instances as a help in designating ushers, for them to wear simple badges made up of a plain gold bar or monogram pin with a modest ribbon attached with suitable words printed on it as "Head Usher," "Assis't Usher," "Usher." This should be in as good taste as possible and should never be worn for mere show.

9. A good deal of responsibility rests on the Head Usher in the matter of enlisting the coöperation of the members of the congregation in exercising general hospitality. This can partially be done by personal work upon his part, assisted by his corps of workers. He should frequently lay this duty upon his helpers and systematically lead them in a campaign to awaken the whole membership.

10. As a help in this hospitality campaign, the Head Usher and all his assistants should

be acquainted with the best literature upon church hospitality. Copies of such should always be kept on hand for circulating among the membership. Some certain book might be chosen for the purpose. Then each one on the ushering force should obtain a copy and make it his business to put it into the hands of the people. Require them each month to report of all whom they have persuaded to read it. In addition to this, the Head Usher might address a circular letter to every member of the church presenting a program of host activities.

There is no limit to the good that may be accomplished if one or two are willing to work. It will take time and energy and perseverance. But remember, " Ye serve the Lord Christ."

(C) STANDARDS OF WORK:

1. Standards count. A high standard plus an honest whole-hearted effort to adhere thereto, in the end, means efficiency. Slipshod methods always mean a mediocre type of service. Why not the best, when it is a possibility? You can have it, namely, a church that cares; a church that is actively true to Christ in its loving expression among and for

its own membership and every stranger within its gates; a church with a corps of ushers so well trained that they know how and never fail to properly exemplify the host spirit within the house of God. This is a possibility for your church. The only question is " What do you actually want? "

2.   The starting place for the Head Usher in this matter of standards of work is with the Head Usher himself. Do not impose standards upon your helpers until you have laid down a worthy one for yourself. Think it through. Determine the part you should play and then hold yourself rigidly to it.

3.   Help your ushers to see the heights of possibility; and then inspire them with desire for attainment. Do more than this. As their leader, see that they do attain. You must hold them to the standard. With friendly tact, yet with firmness, see to it that none of your assistants fall into careless ways. Of course you must guard against a narrow and inflexible discipline. This must be administered in a winning way. Sometimes this will mean that it will be more casual than direct. The greatest good will come, not from constantly deal-

ing with trifles, but by conveying to them inspiration for general and large efficiency.

4. Require faithfulness in their attendance to duties. They should take their work seriously. You will probably have a rule requiring them to report for duty not later than twenty minutes or more before the hour of service. See that this rule is always respected. This is of prime importance and you must be very emphatic in enforcing this regulation. If any of the ushers absent themselves too frequently from their post, or, if knowing that they must be absent, they fail to report it to you in time for securing a substitute, tactfully endeavour to lead them to better habits. If after reasonable effort you fail, it is your duty to replace them with men who will be more faithful.

5. While holding the standard high, do not expect every man to show proficiency at the start. It takes a little time for self-consciousness to wear away and for acquiring all of the principles. However, expect growth and do your part to secure it.

6. You should study each man. Observe the way he does his work. Then in a tactful manner suggest ways of improvement. Do

not be dogmatic in this, but direct him by friendly suggestions. When you are initiating a new man, give him an unstinted amount of your time.

7. Encourage your helpers to study their work. Inspire them to exercise thought. If each man can be brought to have a real desire to bring his own and his associates' work up to the highest standard, your church will soon be known far and wide as a hospitable church. Put them to work trying to solve problems and planning new and better ways of playing the host in the house of God.

8. It might prove of definite value to have several copies of this or some other manual for circulation among them. It would be still better if some way could be provided for giving a copy to each man who assists in the work of ushering. Then for a certain length of time require them to read it through each month.

9. Mention has been made in another place of keeping before your men the evangelistic ideal. This should be interpreted as something more than having the love of Christ in your hearts as you attend to the comfort of your guests; or more than expressing the hope

that in some way they may find Christ. It means that you and your co-workers will do all you can to give Christ to them. This means that as occasion offers, you will speak directly to them of their soul's salvation. Many opportunities will come at the close of evangelistic sermons to say the word that will lead some one to decision. Prepare your men for this. Ask your pastor for the names of some of the best handbooks for personal workers. Secure some copies and encourage their study. Consult with them upon this most important work and then, as Head Usher, set before them a challenging example.

III. *Accountability*

1. In most churches the Head Usher will occupy his position by appointment of some official body of the church; and to this body he is held accountable. This responsible relationship should not be lightly esteemed.

2. Generally, this body will not in any way restrict the activities of the ushers; but if, for any reason, it has seemed best for them to formulate any rules, take pride in closely adhering to them.

3. Where regular or special reports are re-

quired, be prompt in submitting them and take pains in making them accurate and neat.

4. If they lay no special requirements upon you, take it upon yourself to keep them regularly informed as to interesting details of your work. Especially seek their counsel and their approval whenever you are contemplating any new move of importance. Then, if they hesitate to give their approval or if they advise different methods, yield gracefully to their will and judgment.

5. If there be an ushers' association, much responsibility for its success will rest upon you as its first officer. Prove yourself a good leader in this respect.

6. In this matter of accountability, the supreme fact is that you " serve the Lord Christ." Frequently allow the Holy Spirit to search your heart; and, as, by His help, you look into the face of your divine Master, be dissatisfied with anything else from His lips than, " Well done."

III

THE USHERS' ASSOCIATION

I. *What it is*

1. Wherever there are a sufficient number of ushers and of those associated with them as members of the Church Welcome Committee, they should be united in some sort of formal fellowship. The name generally given to such an organization is the Ushers' Association. While a large number may increase interest, profitable association may be formed where the numbers are not many. With even eight or ten faithful members the movement can be made of real worth.

2. In communities where the churches are small an Association can be formed by bringing the ushers of several of the churches together into a common organization. This will prove of great value. The few workers in small churches need inspiration as much as the many in the large churches. While the large church may be sufficient unto itself, the smaller churches can overcome their handicap by unit-

ing their forces. Incidentally, this will be a good developer of the spirit of church union.

3. In cities where a number of churches have their own Associations, a federation between them will strengthen each of them. If rightly directed, such an Association can yield a most effective influence in city-wide movements in the interest of church hospitality. Where such a federation is effected, its plan of organization should not be made so complex, or its meetings held so frequently that it would sap the life of the separate church Associations. Three or four meetings a year will prove ample to make it a real stimulus for the association of each church, while more might be found to be disastrous or at least harmful.

II. *Purpose and Value*

1. The welcoming of guests in the church is largely a matter of heart interest. Individuals can express this, but it has been found that there is a deepening of interest whenever the individual workers are brought close together, not only in a common service but in a mutual fellowship. Fellowship engenders spirit; and spirit stimulates fidelity, quickens desire, and multiplies power for service.

Loyalty is greater when it is the mutual expression of a number of souls bound together in a common mission.

2. Then too, an Ushers' Association helps to keep all the workers actively in the ranks. There are always some who need special incentives to stimulate their interest. They begin well; but sometimes fall by the way. This Association with its social features keeps some of these men attached to the work when other means fail.

3. It likewise provides a place and time for conferences regarding the work the ushers are doing, and serves as a training school for those who are studying the principles of church ushering.

4. It is of value for the impression that it makes upon the church itself. It is a constant reminder of the fact that some of the members are systematically endeavouring to lead the church in the matter of the right reception of its guests. It, therefore, suggests to all the ideal of hospitality.

III. *Organization*

1. It should have the simplest form of organization. There is no need of a lengthy

constitution, or of the multiplication of offices
or committees.

2.   The Head Usher should usually be presi-
dent. The other officers should be elected.

3.   Those eligible for membership are the
Ushers, the Reserves, and those serving by
regular appointment on the Welcome Committee. Every one should be a professing Christian.

4.   A regular time of meeting should be
appointed by the Association. In this day of
committees, clubs, and multiplied social activities it is the part of wisdom not to make these
times too frequent. It is in danger of an early
demise if it be made burdensome. Once a
month, or possibly in some places, once in two
months, will be often enough.

5.   If a suitable room, cozy and attractive
is available in the church, that is where the
meetings should be held. If your church
building offers you no such room or one which
you can make inviting, then some other one
should be secured. Sometimes the best place
will be found in the home of some of its members. The home atmosphere is conducive to
the best work. It stimulates along the very
lines of the usher's work.

IV. *Activities*

1.   At every meeting there should be a conference about the general work. This should be participated in by all and should relate to the progress of their work of ushering. Personal experiences should be exchanged and special problems with which individuals have been confronted should be discussed.

2.   It should be an occasion of inspiration and of positive planning of better things. The Head Usher should come with at least one definite suggestion designated to bring the work up to a higher standard.

3.   Occasionally an outside speaker should be engaged to present some phase of the usher's work and to speak upon the general subject of Church Hospitality.

4.   Elsewhere it has been suggested that each usher be required to read through his manual once a month. It might be well at the Association meetings to have each report whether or not he has observed this rule.

5.   There should always be some attractive social feature. See to it that they have some good wholesome fun. A bit of laughter shared by all; some songs and a cup or two of tea will help to make better ushers of them.

6. If it can be arranged, it might be well to meet about the supper table. At any rate, it will be found to be a capital idea to put on a man-sized banquet once a year. Invite the pastor and his official board. Have some good speeches and a genuine good time. This might conclude with the annual election of officers. Or maybe it would be better to have this meeting follow the election.

7. Establish the organization in mind by having a group photograph taken each year. The men will prize these pictures and it will aid in holding them together.

8. The Association should take a leading part in developing hospitality throughout the general membership of the church. Let it map out definite campaigns and carry them through with system and perseverance.

9. There is no better group than this, in the whole church, to have charge of the Church Socials. These should be held often and wide publicity should be given them, that the attendance may be large. In churches which have a regular social committee appointed by the pastor or official board, it might be feasible for the Ushers' Association to frequently check up its activities. A committee is of

value only when it functions. The ushers should see to it that the social committee does not go to sleep.

10. Many other activities will suggest themselves to those who take the matter seriously in hand. Real thought, believing prayer, and the frequent reminder that in this work they " serve the Lord Christ " will bring ideas, energy, accomplishment, and Divine approval; because, in their service, they have become fellow-helpers to the truth.

IV

THE PASTOR AND GOVERNING BODIES

*It may not be amiss, in a manual such as this
which is primarily addressed to the usher, to
add a word or two for the Pastor and the
Official Board having general oversight over
this part of the church work.*

I. *Attitude Toward the Work*

1. Those who stand back of the ushers
must be convinced that ushering is an important
factor in church work; that it is more
than finding seats for people. They must recognize
the usher to be the official representative
of the congregation in the matter of expressing
the host spirit to all who come to
worship. It is as necessary for you as pastor
and as members of the official board to realize
this as for the usher himself to realize it.

2. Be impressed, especially with the spiritual
significance of this work. Few things
will contribute as much toward the actual spiritual
results of public worship, at least for the
stranger, as a proper atmosphere warmed by
a cordial hospitality. It is Christian service of
a basic and vital nature. It deserves your
deepest consideration.

3. Its importance is so great that you should see to it that adequate provision for it is made for every public service about the church. This means the services of the Lord's Day and all others, not omitting the mid-week prayer meeting. Suppose only one stranger " drops in,"—let it be into a glad welcome.

4. Apart from seeing this work as something very important, you should also recognize that a large share of the responsibility for making it a thing of success rests upon you.

II. *Appointments*

1. Sometimes in small churches no official appointments are made. Some one or two see the need of having ushers and just assume the duty as their own. Of course this is better than not having any one do it; and sometimes the work is well done; but at other times it is far from satisfactory. Regular appointments should always be made, in order that the right individuals may be brought into service and that their services may be vested with the element of accountability.

2. As a rule it will be found advisable for the Board to appoint only the Head Usher,

granting to him the privilege of selecting all of his helpers. If it seems best, you may reserve the right of expressing your approval or disapproval of the same.

3. In this connection it should be observed that such authority as you see fit to delegate to the Head Usher should be respected. Do not go over his head in making suggestions to his appointees, nor in matters of discipline; but work through him.

III. *Standards*

1. If you are to be of real service to your church and of help to the ushers, it is necessary for you to be acquainted with the points of good ushering. Knowledge of some of these you may naturally possess, but some facts may have to be acquired. Fit yourself to be a real adviser. Study the Usher's Manual.

2. Having determined your standards you must see that the ushers are guided by them. It is so easy for slipshod methods to creep in when any work becomes " an old story." The one assurance against this is a faithfully applied standard. This may seem to be a good deal of talk about a small matter; but remember, this is not a small matter. It is Kingdom

work; and the possible returns, of an eternal nature, are great.

3. One of the best ways of standardizing the work, especially along the lines of fidelity upon the part of all participants is by requiring regular reports to be made. It is unnecessary to give any set form for these reports as each church may devise its own suitable to its circumstances.

IV. *Coöperation*

1. This word designates one of the most fruitful facts in human experience. In small undertakings as in large ones, coöperation adds strength for the race and shortens the way to the goal.

2. Frequent consultations with the Head Usher will do him good, if in no other way, by showing him that your eyes are upon his work. Talking things over generally calls forth new ideas that lead to advance steps.

3. A good deal of responsibility has been laid upon the ushers as promulgators of the spirit of hospitality among all the church members. Your coöperation in this is most desirable and necessary. Encourage them to

undertake such a campaign; and then get right back of them and work.

4.   The suggestions made elsewhere in this manual relating to the evangelistic opportunity confronting the ushers may cause some of them to draw back a bit. Yet it is the crowning point of their ministry. If they do hesitate here it will be because of a feeling that they are not qualified for such service. At no point can the pastor be of greater aid than here; and a wise man will he be if he rises to the occasion. Let him explain to them the meaning of this opportunity and inspire them with a love for souls, a desire to win them for Christ, and with a willingness to be used in such work. Practical suggestions should be given and good books on personal work should be placed in their hands. He should then encourage them as individuals to confer with him about the work from week to week and to report to him their various experiences.

5.   Another type of coöperation has to do with furnishing them with proper equipment with which to do their work. No great demands of this nature will be made; and yet some helps may sometimes be needed. Do not count the pennies here.

(*a*) Each usher should have his own manual. It is proper that these be supplied by the Board of Control. Give them to the men, allowing them to retain them as mementos of service when they of necessity give up the work. Keep a supply on hand so that all new recruits may from the start become " thoroughly fur· nished " for their work.

(*b*) If the size of the church warrants it, secure for them the simple badges mentioned in another portion of this manual, to designate them to strangers.

(*c*) Printed leaflets giving information about the church life, its various meetings and public services, the church plant, etc., etc., will prove valuable to give to those guests who manifest special interest. All of the ushers and members of the Welcome Committee should have with them a supply of these whenever they are on duty.

(*d*) It is hard to make a guest comfortable in a room where some of the simple elements of comfort are lacking, viz.: fans, plenty of hymn-books, proper ventilation, special instruments to enable the deaf to hear,[1] etc., etc. Take stock of your special equipment, then

[1] See page 15 for information about Church Acousticon.

make adequate provision. Do not fail here because of a lack of funds. Get busy! Where there is a will there is everything else that is really necessary to properly conduct the work.

6. If there are enough ushers to have an Ushers' Association, see that there is one. Give it all the support it needs for its returns to the church life will be manifold.

7. The easiest kind of coöperation and one of the very best is giving encouragement by word of mouth. Sincere appreciation is not only an effective lubricant, but a marvelous generator of power. How easy to speak the word. See that you do it to your ushers;— and do it often.

8. When all has been said, the one un-paralleled type of coöperation is that which is exercised upon bended knee. God's throne is the place at which to arrange for the success of every feature of the work of the Church. You can pray good ushers into the ranks and you can pray them into better ushers. You can pray your church into the spirit and practice of the warmest kind of friendly hospitality. Do not fail here! On your knees, that souls may be won for the King, through the warm touch of His ambassadors!

INDEX